Karoly Nyisztor

PROTOCOL-ORIENTED PROGRAMMING IN SWIFT 5

Familiarize yourself with POP to fully unleash
the power of Swift 5 and protocols

Contents

I. INTRODUCTION — 2
- 1.1 Overview — 3
- 1.2 What You Should Know — 4
- 1.3 The Exercise Files — 5

II. PROTOCOL-ORIENTED PROGRAMMING FOUNDATIONS — 6
- 2.1 The Paradigm Shift — 7
- 2.2 Protocols — 8
- 2.3 Adopting a Protocol — 12
- 2.4 Adopting Protocols through Extensions — 14
- 2.5 Understanding Polymorphism — 16
- 2.6 Protocol Inheritance — 19
- 2.7 Protocol Composition — 21
- 2.8 Providing Default Behavior in Protocols — 25
- 2.9 Challenge: Removing Tight Coupling — 27
- 2.10 Solution — 30

III. YET ANOTHER PROGRAMMING PARADIGM? — 35
- 3.1 From Unstructured Code to POP — 36
- 3.2 Starting with a Class — 39
- 3.3 Subclassing for a Modular Design — 41
- 3.4 Redesigning Using Protocols — 43
- 3.5 Why Protocols? — 46

IV. PROTOCOLS AND GENERICS — 47
- 4.1 The Importance of Generics — 48
- 4.2 Defining Generic Functions and Methods — 50
- 4.3 Working with Generic Types — 52
- 4.4 Placeholder Types in Protocols — 54
- 4.5 Using Generics with Protocols — 56

4.6 Challenge: Implementing a Generic Stack — 58
4.7 Solution — 59

V. CASE STUDY - IMPLEMENTING AN APP USING POP — 63
5.1 Weather App Design — 64
5.2 Defining the UI Using SwiftUI — 66
5.3 The WebServiceController Protocol — 69
5.4 Working with Third-Party API — 72
5.5 Implementing the OpenWeatherMapController — 73
5.6 Completing the OpenWeatherMapController — 76
5.7 Introducing the ViewModel — 78
5.8 Presenting Weather Data — 80
5.9 Challenge: Adding A Fallback Service — 82
5.10 Solution — 83

CONCLUSION — 86
6.1 Next Steps — 87
6.2 Useful Links — 88

Thank you for joining me on this journey to learn how to take advantage of Protocol-Oriented Programming (in short, POP) to write elegant, professional code.

Programming is a powerful approach that makes it easier to write efficient, elegant, and professional Swift code. Anyone who plans to design, implement, or analyze a modern Swift codebase needs to understand this programming paradigm.

My goal with this book is to make it easy for you to master the crucial protocol-orientation concepts and apply them effectively in your projects.

I'll make the transition from Object-Oriented Programming to Protocol-Oriented Programming as smooth as possible—regardless of whether you've been working with object-oriented languages for decades or you're just about to write your first, extensive project in Swift.

We'll begin with an in-depth discussion of what Protocol-Oriented Programming is and what makes it different from the object-oriented programming approach.

We'll then talk about three fundamental concepts:

- → Protocol extensions
- → Protocol inheritance
- → Protocol composition

Understanding these concepts is crucial to applying the Protocol-Oriented Programming (POP) paradigm effectively. To solidify them, I'm going to lead you through several Swift coding examples.

Although this book focuses on POP, we'll usually encounter generics when using protocols. I dedicated an entire chapter to show you how to leverage the power of generics combined with protocols.

Finally, you can follow along with me as I build a full-blown application from scratch using the protocol-oriented approach.

Throughout the book, you'll acquire coding skills that can be applied in real-world situations. And by the time you finish, you'll have the knowledge to design and write professional applications that leverage the power of protocol-oriented programming.

I. INTRODUCTION

1.1 Overview

Programming(OOP) has become pretty ubiquitous. Software developers use objects and classes all the time; we rely on inheritance to avoid code repetition, protect the sensitive class properties using data hiding, and leverage polymorphism to implement elegant solutions and design patterns. Without a doubt, object orientation is a widely adopted and supported programming paradigm.

Programming provides another level of abstraction on top of OOP. As I'll show you in the upcoming chapters, this new approach can simplify and improve our code considerably.

This book provides an overview of the core concepts in Protocol-Oriented Programming and demonstrates how to apply them effectively using hands-on coding examples.

I'll show you how to eliminate issues plaguing object-oriented systems such as complex class hierarchies and tight-coupling. We'll leverage the power of POP to create granular, change-friendly software systems. We'll employ best-practices and techniques that produce cleaner and less verbose code.

We'll start by comparing object-orientation with protocol-based way software design. This comparative study will help you wrap your head around these new concepts and make it easier to transition to the POP way of thinking.

Next, I'll introduce the main pillars of Protocol-Oriented Programming: protocol extensions, protocol inheritance, and protocol composition. These ideas are crucial, and we're going to build upon them in the rest of the book.

We'll then discuss the why and how of combining generics and protocols.

Finally, we're going to apply the ideas behind the POP paradigm to redesign and improve the design and the code base of an application.

The book also includes several practical challenges (and solutions) that will help you solidify the the concepts.

1.2 What You Should Know

This book aims to deepen your knowledge of protocol-oriented programming techniques and help you build better, more flexible applications.

I'm going to explain all the new concepts and implementation details presented in this book. You don't need to be an expert by any means, but some experience with Swift programming is required. For example, you should know how to work with structures, enumerations, classes, and closures.

Note that I'll be using Xcode running on macOS to implement the code samples in this book. If you're a Mac user, make sure to get Xcode from the Mac App Store. Xcode comes with the latest Swift version, so you don't have to download it separately.

However, you're not restricted to a Mac to follow along with me; any environment that supports compiling and executing Swift 5+ code will do. At the time of writing this book, Swift development is also supported on Windows 10 and various Linux distributions (Ubuntu, CentOS 7, CentOS 8, Amazon Linux 2).

Visit https://swift.org/download/#releases to check out the list of available Swift releases for each supported platform.

1.3 The Exercise Files

This book comes with exercise files that you can use to follow along. Download the repository from https://github.com/nyisztor/pop-swift5 and copy the projects to a dedicated folder.

The demos are organized in folders that match the chapter structure, and each folder contains a "begin" and "end" subfolder. The project in the "begin" folder serves as a starting point if you want to write the code along with me. The "end" folder contains the final, completed project. You can use it to compare your final version to mine.

And with all that said, let's dive in.

II. PROTOCOL-ORIENTED PROGRAMMING FOUNDATIONS

2.1 The Paradigm Shift

At WWDC 2015, Apple announced Swift 2.0, making waves by declaring the programming language would become open-source later that year.

Swift 2.0 included a ton of new language features, including protocol extensions. Apple made it clear that Protocol-Oriented Programing is here to stay, and Swift developers should adopt this development paradigm.

The concept of protocols isn't that new at all—they've been around for decades. Many object-oriented programming languages rely on protocols as a means to define communication contracts between objects.

If you've worked with Java or C#, you've used the term interface instead of protocol. In C++, we've got the abstract class. The creators of Objective-C and Swift decided to use the term "protocol."

These are just different names for the same idea: a protocol/interface/abstract class describes the method and property requirements that need to be implemented by conforming types. From now on, I'll use the term protocol.

Another thing we should get out of the way is that protocols aren't fully functional types. Although we can provide default behavior in protocols, we can't instantiate them - they serve as blueprints rather than concrete types.

Let's continue with a thought experiment. Say we want to design a software system. Following the object-oriented way of thinking, we're inclined to start by identifying the primary entities.

The next step is to model the relationships between these entities. That's when we start creating classes.

Sooner or later, we need to add specialized functionality. That's where inheritance comes into play. Inheritance is one of the pillars of object-oriented programming. However, inheritance comes with severe flaws, as we'll soon see.

Protocols—and protocol inheritance—provide a better alternative to inheritance. The key to this protocol-based approach is to start thinking in terms of protocols rather than classes.

Alright, let's talk about the protocol next.

2.2 Protocols

The fundamental element of protocol-oriented development is—you guessed it—the protocol.

A protocol models abstraction by describing what the conforming types will implement. Rather than defining actual functionality, protocols serve as blueprints.

Let's start by exploring protocol syntax. We'll first declare a protocol as follows:

```
protocol ProtocolName {}
```

Protocol Naming Conventions

Protocol names adhere to the same rules as classes and structures: they must begin with a capital letter and follow upper camel-case notation. Here's a concrete example:

```
protocol BinaryRepresentable {}
```

Protocols that describe what something is should read as nouns—for example, "Collection," "UITableViewDataSource," or "DatabaseWrapper."

Protocols that describe a capability should be named using the suffixes "-able," "-ible," or "-ing," such as "Hashable," "CustomStringConvertible," or "NSCoding."

Protocol naming rules are documented at https://swift.org/documentation/api-design-guidelines/#naming.

Defining Property Requirements

A protocol's method and computed property requirements go between the curly brackets that follow the protocol name. However, unlike for classes and structs, properties declared in a protocol must have at least one getter.

If we declared a property as in the following example:

```
protocol BinaryRepresentable {
    var tag: String
}
```

We'd get an error:

```
"Property in protocol must have explicit {get} or {get set} specifier"
```

We'll make the tag property both settable and gettable by writing get set after its declaration between curly braces:

```
protocol BinaryRepresentable {
    var tag: String {get set}
}
```

Protocols can't require properties to be immutable—using the let keyword would trigger a compiler error. We can, however, define read-only properties by using the var keyword along with the get specifier.

```
var data: Data { get }
```

Note that we can skip the setter, but defining a write-only property requirement is not possible.

> If a property can be set, it needs to have a getter, too.

Protocols let us define type property requirements using the static keyword. The following line defines a static read-only property called counter:

```
static var counter: Int { get }
```

Defining Method Requirements

We can define instance and type method requirements in a protocol. Let's add an instance method called update(), which takes an argument called data of type Data and it returns a Boolean value.

```
func update(data: Data) -> Bool
```

If we define a requirement for a method that modifies the instance, it is recommended to mark it with the mutating keyword. This way, we allow value types to adopt the protocol also.

The update() method is likely to change the instance, so let's mark it as such:

```
mutating func update(data: Data) -> Bool
```

We can also define static method requirements in a protocol using the usual syntax:

```
static func incrementCounter()
```

This method is supposed to increment the internal counter property.

Limiting Conforming Types to Classes

If you want to restrict conforming types to classes only, you can define the protocol as such by making it inherit from the AnyObject protocol.

```
protocol BinaryRepresentable: AnyObject {
    // ...
}
```

After performing this change, Xcode will display an error next to the update() method:

```
"'mutating' method isn't valid on methods in classes or class-
bound protocols"
```

If the protocol should be adopted only by classes, the mutating keyword wouldn't make sense since class methods can always modify the instance. To avoid compiler errors, class-only protocols must not use the mutating keyword.

> Bear in mind that limiting protocols to class types prevents value types from adopting the protocol. Consider carefully before introducing such restrictions.

Let's undo the last change and remove the limitation:

```
protocol BinaryRepresentable {
    // ...
}
```

Defining Initializer Requirements

Protocols can also dictate initializers to be implemented by conforming types. The following initializer requirement takes two arguments: an argument called tag of type String and an argument called data of type Data:

```
init(tag: String, data: Data)
```

The signature is the same as when declaring class initializers, except that we don't provide the initializer's body.

Restrictions

Defining a protocol is quite similar to defining classes or structures, but some restrictions apply. For instance, a protocol can't add immutable property requirements using the let keyword; we can't add default values, computed property, initializer or method definitions either.

And since there's no way to assign default values to the properties defined in a protocol, Swift's type inference engine has no way of working out the type. Therefore, the property types must be provided explicitly.

Now that you know how to create a protocol and define property and method requirements, let's see how we can adopt them.

2.3 Adopting a Protocol

If we want to create a type conforming to a protocol, we must declare and define the matching properties and methods.

Let's create a structure called TaggedData.

```
struct TaggedData {}
```

To make it adopt the BinaryRepresentable protocol, add a colon after the type's name, and write the protocol's name.

```
struct TaggedData: BinaryRepresentable {}
```

After this change, we get a compiler error that says:

```
"Type 'TaggedData' does not conform to protocol 'BinaryRepresent-
able'"
```

We can rely on autocomplete to add the missing property and method declarations. So let's do that. Click the red dot to reveal the details, then click "Fix":

```
BinaryRepresentable {
```

> Type 'TaggedData' does not conform to protocol 'BinaryRepresentable'
> Do you want to add protocol stubs?   Fix

The following code gets generated:

```
struct TaggedData: BinaryRepresentable {
    var tag: String
    var data: Data
    static var counter: Int

    init(tag: String, data: Data) {
        <#code#>
    }

    func update(data: Data) -> Bool {
        <#code#>
    }

    static func incrementCounter() {
        <#code#>
    }
}
```

The implementation is missing, so let's add some code. The initializer should assign a value to the tag and data properties:

```
init(tag: String, data: Data) {
    self.tag = tag
    self.data = data
}
```

The update() method updates the data property and returns true:

```
mutating func update(data: Data) -> Bool {
    self.data = data
    return true
}
```

The method is mutating because it modifies the instance's data property.

The incrementCounter increments the value of the static counter property:

```
static func incrementCounter() {
    counter += 1
}
```

Finally, we need to provide a default value for the static counter instance.

```
static var counter: Int = 0
```

Now the TaggedData type conforms to the BinaryRepresentable protocol and the code should compile without issues.

2.4 Adopting Protocols through Extensions

As developers, we often rely on code that we don't own. We might not even have access to the actual source code, as would be the case when working with Apple's frameworks or other, third-party SDKs.

Let's assume that we're about to build a cryptography framework. We'll follow Apple's recommendation and start with a protocol.

The Encrypting protocol defines a single method requirement:

```swift
protocol Encrypting {
    func xor(key: UInt8) -> Self?
}
```

We can adopt this protocol in our types easily:

```swift
struct TaggedData: Encrypting {
}
```

Xcode even adds the missing protocol stubs for us:

```swift
struct TaggedData: Encrypting {
    func xor(key: UInt8) -> TaggedData? {
        <#code#>
    }
}
```

Now, what if we want to make the String type adopt this protocol? We can't change the implementation of the String structure as we did with the TaggedData type.

```swift
struct String: Encrypting {} // This won't work!
```

However, we can use a type extension to add new methods or properties to an existing type. This approach works even if we don't have access to the specific type's source code.

```swift
extension String: Encrypting {
```

Xcode will generate the method stub for us.

```swift
    func xor(key: UInt8) -> String? {
        <#code#>
    }
```

We can add the implementation next. First, we retrieve the string's contents as a collection of UTF8 codes. The map array method combines each element with the provided key using the XOR (^) operation. Finally, we return a new string built using the encrypted bytes.

```
func xor(key: UInt8) -> String? {
    String(bytes: self.utf8.map { $0 ^ key}, encoding: .utf8)
}
```

Awesome! We just enhanced the String type with a new feature. Let's try it out.

```
let source = "Hello, Protocol!"
let target = source.xor(key: 42)
```

The source variable is the string we want to encode, and target will hold the result of performing the xor method on the source string.

Finally, we print a couple of diagnostic strings.

```
print(target ?? "Failed to encode")
print(target?.xor(key: 42) ?? "Failed to decode.")
```

Executing the playground logs the encrypted and decrypted text in the console:

```
bOFFE
zXE^EIEF
Hello, Protocol!
```

Type extensions let us add protocol requirements to any type, even if we don't have access to its code. That's a useful feature that allows adopting protocols even in types we do not own.

2.5 Understanding Polymorphism

Polymorphism is a well-known concept that also plays an essential role also in Protocol-Oriented Programming.

> The word "polymorphism" comes from Greek and means "many forms." In programming, it denotes the ability to provide a single interface to different types.

To illustrate the concept, let's work through an actual example. We'll start by creating a protocol called Shape. The protocol defines a read-only property requirement.

```
protocol Shape {
    var area: Double { get }
}
```

Next, we'll create several concrete shapes that conform to the Shape protocol. These types must implement the same area property requirement, yet the formula to calculate the area is different for each shape.

The area of a rectangle is the product of its height and width. So, we'll add two additional immutable properties, height and width:

```
struct Rectangle: Shape {
    let height: Double
    let width: Double
    var area: Double {
        return height * width
    }
}
```

We can apply the same formula for a square, but we only need one of the sides because each side has the same length.

```
struct Square: Shape {
    let side: Double
    var area: Double {
        return side * side
    }
}
```

We find the area of a rhombus by multiplying the lengths of the two diagonals and dividing by two. The p and q variables represent the diagonals of the rhombus.

```swift
struct Rhombus: Shape {
    let p: Double
    let q: Double
    var area: Double {
        return (p * q) / 2
    }
}
```

We'll complete our shape arsenal with a circle. The area of a circle is ϖ times its radius squared, where ϖ (pi) is a constant that represents the constant ratio of the circumference of any circle to its diameter:

```swift
struct Circle: Shape {
    let radius: Double

    // A = π * r^2
    var area: Double {
        return .pi * radius * radius
    }
}
```

We're done with the geometry refresher. Now, let's declare a variable of type Shape:

```swift
var shape: Shape
```

Although we could declare it, we cannot instantiate a protocol. We can, however, assign to the shape variable an object of a concrete type that conforms to the Shape protocol. This line will compile without problems:

```swift
shape = Rectangle(height: 10, width: 20)
```

And we use the variable as usual:

```swift
print(shape.area)
```

Next, we'll assign a circle of radius 42 and print its area:

```swift
shape = Circle(radius: 42)
print(shape.area)
```

We can set the shape to a rhombus instance as well:

```swift
shape = Rhombus(p: 4, q: 6)
print(shape.area)
```

To take advantage of the polymorphic behavior, we'll create an array of Shape types:

```
var shapes = [Shape]()
```

We have an empty array that can hold instances of type Shape. Now let's fill the array:

```
shapes.append(Square(side: 10))
shapes.append(Rectangle(height: 5, width: 10))
shapes.append(Rhombus(p: 1, q: 12))
shapes.append(Circle(radius: 3))
```

Will this code work?

An array—just like all the other built-in collections—can only work with a specific type. We can't insert instances of unrelated types into the same array, set, or dictionary.

Yet, these types aren't unrelated. The Rectangle, the Circle, the Square, and the Rhombus conform to the Shape protocol. Thus, the above code is completely valid.

We can iterate through the array using a for-in loop and print each shape's area—even without knowing the actual type:

```
for shape in shapes {
    print(shape.area)
}
```

After executing the playground, the console displays the area of each shape in the array:

```
100.0
50.0
6.0
28.274333882308138
```

Polymorphism allows us to access and use related objects through a common interface without keeping track of their concrete type.

It's a key programming concept that stands at the core of many design patterns. We can rely on polymorphism to build elegant solutions and reduce tight coupling in software systems.

2.6 Protocol Inheritance

A protocol can inherit from one or more protocols and add new requirements on top of the inherited ones—a feature that lets us create granular designs.

Here's the BinaryRepresentable protocol we defined in section 2.2 "Protocols."

```
protocol BinaryRepresentable {
    var tag: String {get}
    var data: Data { get }
    init(tag: String, data: Data)
}
```

Let's assume that we want to add the following requirements:

- → Instances can be persisted locally
- → Instances can be restored later on
- → Ability to retrieve the Base64-encoded version of the data

The first approach would be to define all these requirements in the BinaryRepresentable protocol. However, our protocol would define too many unrelated requirements—and that always indicates a design failure.

The Single Responsibility Principle tells us that a type should have a well-defined purpose, and this principle also applies to protocols.
So, instead of squeezing all these requirements into the same protocol, we'll follow a modular strategy: we'll create dedicated protocols for each functionality.

First, create a protocol that defines the persistence-related requirements:

```
protocol BinaryPersistable: BinaryRepresentable {
```

The BinaryPersistable protocol inherits from BinaryRepresentable. Types that adopt the BinaryPersistable protocol have to implement the property and method requirements from both protocols.

BinaryPersistable adds an initializer requirement that is responsible for loading a previously saved instance from the storage.

The initializer takes a tag argument of type String. This argument identifies the instance to be restored. The contentsOf parameter represents the location URL.

We may face various issues when dealing with persistence: missing files, lack of permission, and so on. So it's a good idea to mark the initializer as "throwable" using the throws keyword.

```
protocol BinaryPersistable: BinaryRepresentable {
    init(tag: String, contentsOf url: URL) throws
```

Next, we'll declare the persist() method responsible for the restoration functionality. The method takes a url parameter that represents the storage location. Again, since we're dealing with persistence, we mark it as throwable.

```
    func persist(to url: URL) throws
```

Protocol inheritance is similar to class inheritance. However, Swift protocols aren't limited to single inheritance. We could add further requirements to adopters of BinaryPersistable, such as CustomStringConvertible or Equatable:

```
protocol BinaryPersistable: BinaryRepresentable, CustomStringConvertible, Equatable {
    // ...
}
```

A type that conforms to BinaryPersistable needs to implement the requirements for BinaryRepresentable, CustomStringConvertible, Equatable, and BinaryPersistable as well.

Next, we create a protocol for the Base64-encoding:

```
protocol Base64Encodable: BinaryRepresentable {}
```

The Base64Encodable protocol defines a single, read-only property requirement called base64:

```
protocol Base64Encodable: BinaryRepresentable {
    var base64: String { get }
}
```

Conforming types can decide which protocol to adopt:

- → BinaryRepresentable, if it only needs to hold data along with an identifier.
- → BinaryPersistable, if it requires persistence capabilities
- → Base64Encodable, if retrieving the Base64-encoded string representation of its data is a feature we need.

Types are not limited to conforming to a single protocol. Developers can decide to create classes or value types that adopt two or all three protocols.

2.7 Protocol Composition

Swift, like many other programming languages, doesn't allow multiple inheritance for classes. However, any type can adopt multiple protocols.

Protocol composition is a fundamental idea in protocol-oriented programming. By conforming to multiple protocols, we can ensure that our types implement the requirements they need, without inheriting unnecessary noise from a class hierarchy.

I'm going to walk you through an actual coding example to demonstrate how it works. First, create a structure called MyData:

```
struct MyData {}
```

Let's assume that it has to support persistence and Base64 encoding. All we need to do is make it adopt both the BinaryPersistable and Base64Encodable protocols:

```
struct MyData: BinaryPersistable, Base64Encodable {}
```

Xcode can generate the protocol stubs for us.

```
struct MyData: BinaryPersistable, Base64Encodable {
    init(tag: String, contentsOf url: URL) throws {
        
    }
    
    func persist(to url: URL) throws {
        <#code#>
    }
    
    var base64: String
    var tag: String
    var data: Data
    
    init(tag: String, data: Data) {
        <#code#>
    }
}
```

Next, we'll implement the initializer. We'll declare a data variable and initialize it using Data.init(contentsOf: url). This initializer can throw an error. Thus, we need to call it using the try keyword. Then, call self.init by passing in the tag and the data as arguments:

```swift
init(tag: String, contentsOf url: URL) throws {
    let data = try Data.init(contentsOf: url)
    self.init(tag: tag, data: data)
}
```

The persist() method uses the write(to:) Data instance method to write the contents to the location provided by the url argument. It's a throwable method, so we call it using try:

```swift
func persist(to url: URL) throws {
    try self.data.write(to: url)
}
```

The base64 property returns the Base64-encoded string representation of the data:

```swift
var base64: String {
    self.data.base64EncodedString()
}
```

Finally, let's implement the default initializer:

```swift
init(tag: String, data: Data) {
    self.tag = tag
    self.data = data
}
```

Now, let's add a custom description by adopting the CustomStringConvertible protocol:

```swift
struct MyData: BinaryPersistable, Base64Encodable, CustomString-
Convertible {
```

The CustomStringConvertible protocol defines a description property requirement.

```swift
var description: String
```

The implementation is straightforward - we'll return a string containing the type's name and tag property.

```swift
var description: String {
    "MyData(\(tag))"
}
```

The MyData structure now conforms to multiple protocols: BinaryRepresentable, BinaryPersistable, Base64Encodable, and CustomStringConvertible.

We can add as many protocols to the type inheritance list as we need. However, as we adopt new protocols, the type's implementation keeps growing, making it increasingly difficult to parse and maintain the code.

Let's refactor our structure. We'll introduce a dedicated type extension for each protocol conformance.

> Swift's type extension feature can help us improve code readability and better organize our code.

First, we'll create a dedicated extension for the CustomStringConvertible conformance:

```
extension MyData: CustomStringConvertible {}
```

Now we can move the definition of the description property from the structure to the extension:

```
extension MyData: CustomStringConvertible {
    var description: String {
        "MyData(\(tag))"
    }
}
```

Next, we'll remove the protocol conformance from the structure's inheritance list.

```
struct MyData: BinaryPersistable, Base64Encodable {
```

Similarly, we create an extension for the conformance to Base64Encodable. We'll move the base64 property to this extension:

```
extension MyData: Base64Encodable {
    var base64: String {
        self.data.base64EncodedString()
    }
}
```

Now, we can delete Base64Encodable from MyData's inheritance list.

```
struct MyData: BinaryPersistable {
```

Finally, we'll define an extension for the BinaryPersistable conformance and move over the initializer and the persist() method:

```
extension MyData: BinaryPersistable {
```

```
    init(tag: String, contentsOf url: URL) throws {
        let data = try Data.init(contentsOf: url)
        self.init(tag: tag, data: data)
    }

    func persist(to url: URL) throws {
        try self.data.write(to: url)
    }
}
```

After this change, we can also remove the last protocol from the inheritance list:

```
struct MyData:  {
    var tag: String
    var data: Data
    init(tag: String, data: Data) {
        self.tag = tag
        self.data = data
    }
}
```

This MyData structure's implementation is cleaner, yet we kept all the features, and our code is better organized and easier to follow.

2.8 Providing Default Behavior in Protocols

Providing default behavior in the protocol could save us a lot of typing when implementing the conforming types.

Although we can't include implementation in the protocol's body, it is possible to provide default method and property implementations in a protocol extension.

Let's first provide default implementations for the BinaryPersistable protocol. We declare protocol extensions using the extension keyword. It's the same syntax we used to create type extensions.

```
extension BinaryPersistable {}
```

After creating the extension, we can move the method definitions from the corresponding MyData extension:

```
extension BinaryPersistable {
    init(tag: String, contentsOf url: URL) throws {
        let data = try Data.init(contentsOf: url)
        self.init(tag: tag, data: data)
    }

    func persist(to url: URL) throws {
        try self.data.write(to: url)
    }
}
```

We'll provide the default implementation for Base64Encodable in a similar vein: we'll copy the base64 property's definition from the MyData: Base64Encodable extension:

```
extension Base64Encodable {
    var base64: String {
        self.data.base64EncodedString()
    }
}
```

With our extensions in place, conforming types don't need to implement the property or method requirements. These will be available through the protocol extensions.

The MyData: Base64Encodable and MyData: BinaryPersistable extensions have become redundant. Thus, we can safely delete them.

However, we need to add back the two protocols to the inheritance list:

```
struct MyData: BinaryPersistable, Base64Encodable {}
```

The code should compile without errors.

We can create new types that adopt these protocols with only a few lines of code. Here's how to define a structure that conforms to the BinaryPersistable protocol:

```
struct PersistableData: BinaryPersistable {
    var tag: String
    var data: Data
}
```

It couldn't be simpler, right?

Providing default implementations for methods and computed properties through protocol extensions can simplify the code of the adopting types to a great extent. Note that conforming types can still override the default behavior defined in the protocol extension.

2.9 Challenge: Removing Tight Coupling

Here's a coding challenge to help you solidify the concepts presented in this chapter.

In this program, we have a PaymentController class that declares two properties, amazonService and etsyService. The class has an initializer and a method that calculates the earnings made on Amazon and Etsy.

```
class PaymentController {
    let amazonService: AmazonService
    let etsyService: EtsyService

    init(amazon: AmazonService, etsy: EtsyService) {
        amazonService = amazon
        etsyService = etsy
    }

    func calculateEarnings() -> Float {
        amazonService.earnings + etsyService.totalSold
    }
}
```

The AmazonService and the EtsyService types are defined in the Services.swift file.

Their implementation is straightforward: whenever we sell something on a given platform, the profit gets added to a private 'balance' variable. AmazonService exposes orderPlaced(), and EtsyService has the method itemSold() for this purpose.

Each class has a property that returns the total profit (totalSold).

```
public class AmazonService {
    private var balance: Float = 0

    public init() {}

    public func orderPlaced(payment: Float) {
        balance += payment
    }

    public var earnings: Float {
        balance
    }
}
```

```swift
public class EtsyService {
    private var earnings: Float = 0

    public init() {}

    public func itemSold(profit: Float) {
        earnings += profit
    }

    public var totalSold: Float {
        earnings
    }
}
```

In the main playground file, we've instantiated an AmazonService and an EtsyService:

```swift
let amazonService = AmazonService()
let etsyService = EtsyService()
```

These instances are then passed to the PaymentController initializer.

```swift
let controller = PaymentController(amazon: amazonService,
                                   etsy: etsyService)
```

We simulate sales by calling the corresponding service methods.

```swift
amazonService.orderPlaced(payment: 100)
etsyService.itemSold(profit: 25)
amazonService.orderPlaced(payment: 12.50)
```

Finally, we print the total profit by calling the controller's calculateEarnings() method:

```swift
print("Total earned: \(controller.calculateEarnings())")
```

This code works, yet the current design shows a serious weakness: the PaymentController class references the AmazonService and the EtsyService types directly.
That's a sign of tight coupling, which can become a severe issue if we don't stop it from spreading.

To illustrate the problem, imagine that we need to modify the AmazonService type's public API. As a result, we'd also need to refactor the PaymentController's code. The maintenance effort will increase as we include additional services.

Let's try to reduce the coupling by removing the dependencies between the

PaymentController and the concrete service types. Instead of relying on the AmazonService and EtsyService type directly, we'll introduce a level of abstraction.

There are different ways to solve this problem. Here are a few hints:

- → Introduce a public Service protocol and define the property and method requirements
- → Adopt the protocol by declaring AmazonService and EtsyService type extensions
- → Hide the concrete types by changing their visibility levels
- → Create a factory method that returns a Service protocol based on an identifier
- → Optionally, you can embed the factory method in a helper type
- → Remove the concrete service type references from the PaymentController. Instead, rely on the Service protocol.

You should stop here and download the exercise files. Start making the necessary changes, and proceed to the next section once you've implemented your solution—or if you get stuck.

Good luck!

2.10 Solution

How did it go? Did you manage to get rid of the tight coupling between the PaymentController and the AmazonService and EtsyService classes?

Here's one way to fix this problem. Let's take another look at the two service classes:

```
public class AmazonService {
    private var balance: Float = 0

    public init() {}

    public func orderPlaced(payment: Float) {
        balance += payment
    }

    public var earnings: Float {
        balance
    }
}

public class EtsyService {
    private var earnings: Float = 0

    public init() {}

    public func itemSold(profit: Float) {
        earnings += profit
    }

    public var totalSold: Float {
        earnings
    }
}
```

Both classes define the same functionality. They differ only in their property and method names.

We could create a common protocol that defines these requirements. Thus, we introduce a level of abstraction—the first logical step toward a loosely coupled system.

So, let's create a public protocol called Service:

```
public protocol Service {}
```

We're going to declare the property that represents the total profit first. total is of type float, and it is read-only since we don't want callers to modify it directly:

```
public protocol Service {
    var total: Float {get}
}
```

Next comes the add() method, which increases the total by the amount provided in the payment argument. We declare it as mutating since it modifies the instance, and we don't want to exclude value types:

```
    mutating func add(payment: Float)
}
```

We'll make the AmazonService and EtsyService classes adopt the protocol using type extensions:

```
extension AmazonService: Service {
```

total returns the value of the earnings property. The add() method delegates the call to the orderPlaced() method:

```
    public var total: Float {
        earnings
    }

    public func add(payment: Float) {
        orderPlaced(payment: payment)
    }
}
```

Similarly, we create an extension for EtsyService - and adopt the Service protocol:

```
extension EtsyService: Service {
```

total returns the value totalSold:

```
    public var total: Float {
        totalSold
    }
```

The add() method invokes itemSold():

```
    public func add(payment: Float) {
        itemSold(profit: payment)
    }
}
```

Now we can hide the concrete service types. We're going to change their visibility levels to private. The class and all its public properties and methods should be private, except for the initializer. The initializer will be fileprivate because it will be invoked from the factory method.

```
private class AmazonService {
    private var balance: Float = 0

    fileprivate init() {}

    private func orderPlaced(payment: Float) {
        balance += payment
    }

    private var earnings: Float {
        balance
    }
}
```

Let's also change the visibility of EtsyService:

```
private class EtsyService {
    private var earnings: Float = 0

    fileprivate init() {}

    private func itemSold(profit: Float) {
        earnings += profit
    }

    private var totalSold: Float {
        earnings
    }
}
```

Since the service types are private, trying to build the program would trigger a compile error.

We can fix this problem easily. In the Services.swift file, we'll declare a public enumeration called ServiceType wth two cases: amazon and etsy. We'll use these values to identify the concrete service types in the factory method:

```
public enum ServiceType {
    case amazon
    case etsy
}
```

We'll implement the factory method next. make() takes a single parameter, 'service' of type ServiceType. The return type is the Service protocol. Clients won't deal with the AmazonService or EtsyService classes. They only see the ServiceType enumeration and the Service protocol.

```
public func make(service: ServiceType) -> Service {
    switch service {
    case .amazon:
        return AmazonService()
    case .etsy:
        return EtsyService()
    }
}
```

We'll refactor the PaymentController next. First, we'll remove the obsolete AmazonService and EtsyService references.

We'll declare a property that holds the list of services instead--an array of Service types. Thus, we're relying on the protocol, and not the concrete service types.

We'll also update the initializer. It takes a parameter of type array of Service and it assigns it to the services property:

```
class PaymentController {
    let services: [Service]

    init(services: [Service]) {
        self.services = services
    }

    func calculateEarnings() -> Float {
        amazonService.earnings + etsyService.totalSold
    }
}
```

The calculateEarnings() method comes next. We'll iterate through the items of the elements from the services array and sum up the value of their total property:

```
    func calculateEarnings() -> Float {
        var result: Float = 0
        services.forEach { (service) in
            result += service.total
        }
        return result
    }
```

Alternatively, we can use the reduce() array method which shrinks the implementation to one line of code:

```
func calculateEarnings() -> Float {
    services.reduce(0) { $0 + $1.total}
}
```

Here's how it works. The initial result is 0. In the closure, we calculate the sum of the previous call's return value ($0) and the next element's 'total' property ($1.total).

From now on, we'll use the factory method instead of instantiating the AmazonService and EtsyService classes:

```
var amazonService = make(service: .amazon) //AmazonService()
var etsyService = make(service: .etsy) //EtsyService()
```

Finally, we'll need to update the initialization of the PaymentController, too:

```
let controller = PaymentController(services: [amazonService, etsy-
Service])
```

The code builds and runs without issues, and we should see the same results as before.

The new design is loosely coupled and flexible. The PaymentController relies on the common protocol. Since it doesn't have dependencies on any of the actual service classes, changing AmazonService or EtsyService doesn't affect the PaymentController.

On top of that, integrating new services is easy. The new types need to adopt the Service protocol, and we have to include the new cases into the ServiceType enumeration and maintain the factory method.

III. YET ANOTHER PROGRAMMING PARADIGM?

3.1 From Unstructured Code to POP

Do we really need yet another programming paradigm? To answer this question, we need to take a step back and have a look at the evolution of computer programming.

1950	1960	1980
Non-structured programming	Structured programming	Object-Oriented programming

Non-structured programming

It all started around 1950, and it took about ten years to develop the first programming languages: Fortran, Cobol, and Algol.

Back then, there were no fancy IDEs or text editors; they wouldn't have been of much use since there were no displays either.

Programmers coded their programs on special sheets of paper called coding sheets. The following example shows a COBOL Coding Sheet:

```
00201        DATA RECORD IS RECORD-IN.
00202    01  RECORD-IN.
00203        05  STUDENT-NAME-IN      PIC X(20).
00204        05  STUDENT-CLASS-IN     PIC 9.
00205        05  GRADE-1              PIC 9.
00206        05  GRADE-2              PIC 9.
00207        05  GRADE-3              PIC 9.
00208    FD  FILE-OUT
00209        LABEL RECORDS ARE OMITTED
00210        DATA RECORD IS RECORD-OUT.
00211    01  RECORD-OUT.
00212        05  STUDENT-NAME-OUT     PIC X(20).
00213        05  FILLER               PIC X(5)   VALUE SPACES.
00214        05  AVERAGE-GRADE-OUT    PIC 9.99.
00215    WORKING-STORAGE SECTION.
00216    77  EOF                      PIC 9      VALUE 0.
00217    77  TOTAL-GRD                PIC 99.
00218    PROCEDURE DIVISION.
00219    GPA-REPORT.
00220    *1.0 START
```

That's how programmers wrote their code until the mid-1970s. The sheets were taken by operators whose job was to punch the instructions onto a punched card using a keypunch machine.

Here's an image of a punched card:

```
//STEP2 EXEC PROC=SLINK, TESTPGM=BADK,ACCT=BADK
 ▪  ▪ ▪▪    ▪  ▪     ▪  ▪ ▪▪▪   ▪▪▪  ▪▪▪
    ▪      ▪▪▪  ▪ ▪▪        ▪▪  ▪           ▪
▪▪▪▪00000▪0000000▪▪000000▪0▪▪000▪00000000▪▪000000000000000000000000000000000
▪▪111111111111111111111111111111▪111▪11111▪1111111111111111111111111111111111
22▪222▪22222222222▪222▪2222▪22222▪22▪222222▪22▪22222222222222222222222222222222
333▪3333333▪3333▪33▪33333▪33▪3333333333▪▪▪3333333333333333333333333333333333333
4444444444444444444444444444444▪444▪44444444▪4444444444444444444444444444444444
5555▪555▪5▪555555▪555▪5555▪55555▪555555555▪55555555555555555555555555555555555
666666666666666▪6666666666666666666666666666666666666666666666666666666666666
77777▪777▪777▪7777777777777▪▪7777777777777777777777777777777777777777777777777
8888888888888888▪888888888888888▪8888888▪8888888888888888888888888888888888888
```

If the operator made a single mistake, the entire card had to be re-punched.

Later the punch cards were converted to magnetic type files that could be stored more efficiently.

Initially, computer programs were big, contiguous chunks of code. Unstructured programming was the earliest programming paradigm. The code consisted of sequentially-ordered instructions. Each statement would go in a new line. Source code lines were numbered or identified by a label.

The following Sinclair Basic code snippet converts from Fahrenheit to Celsius degrees:

```
10 PRINT "Fahrenheit", "Celsius"
20 PRINT
30 INPUT "Enter deg F", F
40 PRINT F, (F-32)*5/9
50 GO TO 30
```

As the programs grew in complexity, the drawbacks of this approach became apparent. Maintaining or even understanding such a codebase was challenging. To make any changes or improvements, you had to check the statements line by line.

This task becomes overwhelming as the number of code lines increases. Non-structured programming has received much criticism for producing complicated, difficult-to-understand, and almost impossible-to-maintain code.

Structured Programming

Structured programming emerged in the late 50s. Structured programming languages break down code into logical steps. They rely on subroutines or functions, which contain a set of instructions to be carried out.

Structured programming was a significant improvement compared to monolithic coding practices. The introduction of named functions improved the readability of computer programs and reduced development times substantially.

Even with the improved quality, developers started to face new challenges. The weaknesses of structured programming started to surface as programs grew in complexity.

Object-Oriented Programming

Object orientation--the next big step in the evolution of programming paradigms--appeared in the 1980s.

Object orientation aims to bring the world of programming closer to the real world.

The main idea was to split apart the program into self-contained objects that interact with each other. Each object represents a part of the system that gets mapped to a distinct entity. An object functions as a separate program in and of itself; it operates on its own data and has a specific role.

3.2 Starting with a Class

Let's go ahead and do some actual coding. We'll assume that we need to create types that fulfill the following requirements:

- → Store data along with a key
- → Provide persistence capabilities
- → Allow retrieving the Base64-encoded representation of the data

Switch over to Xcode if you wan to follow along with me. We'll start with a class called TaggedData:

```
class TaggedData {
```

We'll add two properties that represent the identifier: the tag property of type String, and the data property of type Data.

```
    var tag: String
    var data: Data
```

We also need to implement the initializer:

```
    init(tag: String, data: Data) {
        self.tag = tag
        self.data = data
    }
```

We just fulfilled the first requirement: we have a type that can store data along with an identifier.

Now, let's add the local persistence feature. The persist() method writes the contents of the data to the location specified by the url argument:

```
    func persist(to url: URL) throws {
        try self.data.write(to: url)
    }
```

We'll create a convenience initializer to load the data from persistence. The initializer takes two parameters: the tag and the url that represents the storage location. We mark it with the throws keyword because it relies on a method that can throw an error.

The initializer loads the data from the URL using the Data type's init(contentsOf:) method. This method might throw an error, so we call it using try.

If we get a valid data object, we call the TaggedData initializer with the tag and the data arguments.

```
convenience init(tag: String, contentsOf url: URL) throws {
    let data = try Data(contentsOf: url)
    self.init(tag: tag, data: data)
}
```

Finally, we add a computed property that returns the Base64-encoded string representation of the data:

```
var base64EncodedString: String {
    data.base64EncodedString()
}
```

And with that, we've implemented all the requirements. But do we deserve a pat on the back?

Now, while this approach works, it goes against the Single Responsibility Principle, one of the five basic software engineering principles known as SOLID.

> The Single Responsibility Principle states that "every class should have responsibility over a single part of the functionality provided by the software, and that responsibility should be entirely encapsulated by the class."

A class should have one well-defined purpose. However, our TaggedData class does more than one thing:

- → Holds data along with a unique identifier
- → Stores and loads data from the filesystem
- → Returns the Base64-encoded representation of the data

A type with too many responsibilities is often called a 'God' object. As more and more types depend on the God object, the system becomes tightly coupled, which in turn is a sure-fire sign of bad design.

We need to find a better way to fulfill the requirements.

3.3 Subclassing for a Modular Design

Starting with a class that implements all requirements leads to the so-called God object, a class that has too many responsibilities.

Having such classes introduces tight coupling, a severe "disease" of object-oriented systems. As more and more objects depend on each other, code changes will tend to spread across the codebase. Fixing bugs or adding new features becomes a tedious, error-prone task.

We're going to refactor the TaggedData class and break out some of the functionality into subclasses.

Let's simplify the TaggedData class by getting rid of everything except for the two properties and the initializer.

```swift
class TaggedData {
    var tag: String
    var data: Data

    init(tag: String, data: Data) {
        self.tag = tag
        self.data = data
    }
}
```

Now the class has a single, well-defined responsibility: it holds data that can be identified using a tag.

Next, we'll implement the local persistence feature in a subclass called PersistentTaggedData. This subclass defines the persist() and the convenience initializer methods.

```swift
class PersistentTaggedData: TaggedData {
    func persist(to url: URL) throws {
        try self.data.write(to: url)
    }

    convenience init(tag: String, contentsOf url: URL) throws {
        let data = try Data(contentsOf: url)
        self.init(tag: tag, data: data)
    }
}
```

Again, we end up with a class that has one responsibility: it handles data persistence.

Finally, we'll implement the Base64-encoding feature. We'll create yet another TaggedData subclass called TaggedDataWithEncoding:

```
class TaggedDataWithEncoding: TaggedData {
    var base64EncodedString: String {
        data.base64EncodedString()
    }
}
```

We just revamped our original design.

Instead of a monolithic TaggedData class, we now have separate subclasses, with well-defined responsibilities. We have a modular design, that adheres to the Single Responsibility Principle.

However, there are further issues with this code. As we add new requirements, the number of subclasses increases, leading to type explosion, another common pitfall of object-oriented systems. Besides, subclassing doesn't work with value types.

Luckily, protocols are here to save the day!

3.4 Redesigning Using Protocols

Subclassing helped us solve the God-object problem, and we managed to come up with a more granular design. However, we're now facing two new challenges:

- → inheritance doesn't work with value types
- → subclassing might lead to type explosion

We'll revamp our design using protocols. Instead of working with classes, we'll create dedicated protocols for each major feature. To recap, we need to fulfill the following requirements:

- → Store data along with a key
- → Provide persistence capabilities
- → Retrieve the Base64-encoded representation of the data

The first protocol declares the key-data storage requirements:

```
protocol TaggedData {
    var tag: String { get set }
    var data: Data { get set }
    init(tag: String, data: Data)
}
```

The TaggedData protocol declares the tag and data property requirements. Both properties are gettable and settable. The protocol also declares an initializer requirement. Conforming types must implement both properties and the initializer.

Next, we'll create a protocol that declares the requirements needed to persist the data. This protocol describes a capability. To adhere to Swift naming rules, let's name it TaggedDataPersisting. The protocol declares the initializer and the persist() method requirement for data storage.

```
protocol TaggedDataPersisting: TaggedData {
    init(tag: String, contentsOf url: URL) throws
    func persist(to url: URL) throws
}
```

The third protocol declares the Base64-encoding requirements. TaggedDataEncoding declares a single, read-only property requirement.

```
protocol TaggedDataEncoding: TaggedData {
    var base64Encoded: String { get }
}
```

We've got three protocols, but they don't define the actual functionality. Conforming types will have to implement the missing logic.

To avoid code redundancy, we can provide default behavior to any method or computed property requirement of a protocol using protocol extensions.

First, we'll define the default implementation for the TaggedDataPersisting protocol methods:

```swift
extension TaggedDataPersisting {
    init(tag: String, contentsOf url: URL) throws {
        let data = try Data(contentsOf: url)
        self.init(tag: tag, data: data)
    }

    func persist(to url: URL) throws {
        try self.data.write(to: url)
    }
}
```

The code is the same that we used in our class-based example.

Next, we'll define the default behavior for the TaggedDataEncoding's base64Encoded property declaration:

```swift
extension TaggedDataEncoding {
    var base64Encoded: String {
        data.base64EncodedString()
    }
}
```

Adopting any or all of these protocols is straightforward. Assuming that we need a type that encapsulates some data and a key, we'd write the following:

```swift
class MyTaggedData: TaggedData {
    var tag: String
    var data: Data

    required init(tag: String, data: Data) {
        self.tag = tag
        self.data = data
    }
}
```

Simple enough! Plus, protocols can be also adopted by value types. We can skip the initializer since member-wise initializers get automatically generated for structures:

```
struct MyTaggedData: TaggedData {
    var tag: String
    var data: Data
}
```

We can instantiate the new type as usual:

```
let taggedData = MyTaggedData(tag: "first",
                              data: Data(repeating: 0, count: 1))
```

If the type needs persistence features, we can make it conform to the TaggedDataPersisting protocol. Note that we don't have to define protocol methods because we've provided a default implementation already.

```
struct MyTaggedData: TaggedDataPersisting {
    var tag: String
    var data: Data
}
```

After creating a MyTaggedData object, we can use the data persistence feature:

```
let taggedData = MyTaggedData(tag: "42",
        data: Data(repeating: 42, count: 1))

let documentsURL = FileManager.default.urls(for: .documentDirectory, in: .userDomainMask)[0]
let url = documentsURL.appendingPathComponent("tagged")

try? taggedData.persist(to: url)
```

To support Base64-encoding, we include TaggedDataEncoding in the protocol conformance list:

```
struct MyTaggedData: TaggedDataPersisting, TaggedDataEncoding {
```

The Base64-encoding functionality works right away:

```
let str = taggedData.base64Encoded
```

Our type supports data persistence and Base64 encoding without any additional coding. All we need is to make our types adopt the TaggedDataPersisting or TaggedDataEncoding protocols—or both if we need all the features.

The Protocol-orieted design lead to a better and more flexible system. Plus, we avoided all the pitfalls of the class-based solutions.

3.5 Why Protocols?

Protocols and protocol inheritance are a superior and more flexible way of designing our software systems than the class-based approach.

That's because modeling an abstraction using classes implies inheritance. Although inheritance has been around for a while, it doesn't come without pitfalls and restrictions. Let's have a look at both the benefits and the drawbacks of this fundamental object-oriented concept.

In a classic object-oriented design, the superclass provides the core functionality. It includes all the logic required to satisfy the requirements for a type. If we need different behavior, we can add subclasses.

A subclass can:

- → Use the behavior defined in the superclass
- → Completely override the behavior from the superclass
- → Or use some of the default behavior provided by the base class

Although inheritance gives us a lot of flexibility and freedom, it also has some severe limitations.

Limitation #1

Swift, like many other programming languages, prohibits multiple inheritance. Thus, if a subclass needs functionality from another superclass, we can't make it work. We could add that feature to our superclass, but that strategy leads to the God-object issue we saw earlier.

Limitation #2

Inheritance only works with reference types—a severe limitation, especially considering that value types have become first-class citizens in Swift.

Protocols solve all of these issues. Although Swift restricts multiple inheritance, any type can implement multiple protocols. That allows for granular designs by creating as many protocols as needed. Additionally, we're not restricted to classes since value types can also conform to protocols.

By adopting multiple protocols, we can create types that fulfill all necessary requirements. Default implementations eliminate or reduce the amount of client code significantly.

IV. PROTOCOLS AND GENERICS

4.1 The Importance of Generics

Generics are deeply rooted in the Swift programming language, and they are essential when it comes to Protocol-Oriented development as well.

Whenever we encounter protocols, we'll often also see generics. The built-in Swift collection types are a good example—they conform to the Collection protocol and several other protocols as well. Additionally, the Dictionary, the Array, and the Set are all defined as generic types.

Generics can save us from typing similar code over and over again. Let me show you what that means through a practical example.

Assume that we need a function that tells whether two values are equal. We could come up with the following solution.

```
func equals(lhs: Int, rhs: Int) -> Bool {
    return lhs == rhs
}
```

This implementation is straightforward and it works as expected:

```
print(equals(lhs: 3, rhs: 4))
```

However, our function has a severe limitation: we can't use it to compare two Double values.

```
print(equals(lhs: 1.4, rhs: 1.5))
```

We get the following compiler error:

```
Cannot convert value of type 'Double' to expected argument type 'Int'
```

No problem, we can define a new function that works with Double types:

```
func equals(lhs: Double, rhs: Double) -> Bool {
    return lhs == rhs
}
```

So far we've covered Int and Double. How about the following:

```
let pi: Float = 3.14
let e: Float = 2.71

print(equals(lhs: pi, rhs: e))
```

Note that Swift infers floating-point numbers to Double (rather than Float). That's why we need to specify the Float type explicitly.

Again, we get a compiler error:

```
Cannot invoke 'equals' with an argument list of type '(lhs: Float, rhs: Float)
```

We end up creating yet another function that accepts Float types:

```
func equals(lhs: Float, rhs: Float) -> Bool {
    return lhs == rhs
}
```

By now, you've probably noticed an emerging pattern: we need to implement a dedicated equals() function for each new type we want to compare, which leads to many similar functions and a lot of redundant code.

This strategy goes against the Don't Repeat Yourself (DRY) principle, which states that we should eliminate duplication in logic via abstraction.

And that's precisely the problem that generics solve.

4.2 Defining Generic Functions and Methods

Implementing a new function for every type leads to a lot of redundant code. To avoid code duplication, we can combine all the different functions into a single generic function.

To create a generic function, we need to provide at least one placeholder type. The placeholder must appear right after the function's name between angle brackets.

```
func equals<T>
```

We could use any other identifier—capital T is just a popular way to refer to generic placeholders.

We can refer to this placeholder type in the argument list or anywhere in the function's body as in the following example:

```
func equals<T>(lhs: T, rhs: T) -> Bool
```

The left-hand side parameter is of type T, and we also use the placeholder type for the second parameter. The function returns a Boolean value.

The implementation part is straightforward: we return the result of comparing the two arguments:

```
func equals<T>(lhs: T, rhs: T) -> Bool {
    return lhs == rhs
}
```

If we tried to compile this code, we'd get an error:

```
Binary operator '==' cannot be applied to two 'T' operands
```

Swift doesn't know how to compare the two objects of placeholder type. A type needs to conform to the Equatable protocol to test whether its instances are equal.

We can enforce this requirement by applying a type constraint on the placeholder type. A type constraint specifies that the type conforms to a particular protocol or inherits from a specific class. So, let's apply the type constraint.

```
func equals<T: Equatable>(lhs: T, rhs: T) -> Bool {
```

The syntax is simple: we place a constraint after the placeholder separated by a colon.

Now the function accepts instances of types that adopt the Equatable protocol.

Most basic built-in Swift types conform to the Equatable protocol, and the String type is one of them. So, the function should work with String instances. Let's give it a try by comparing two strings:

```
equals(lhs: "abcd", rhs: "dcba")
```

This line should evaluate to "false."

Next, we compare two double values:

```
equals(lhs: Double.pi, rhs: 3.14)
```

The function returns false because Double.pi has higher precision than the right-hand argument.

We can pass in Data instances to the equals function:

```
let d1 = Data(repeating: 1, count: 10)
let d2 = Data(repeating: 1, count: 10)
equals(lhs: d1, rhs: d2)
```

The Data(repeating:, count:) initializer creates a data object using a repeating byte pattern. The function returns true because the two data instances have the same contents.

Our generic function works with most basic types from the Swift standard library, as they conform to the Equatable protocol.

Generic functions prevent cluttering our code with functions that only differ by the type of their parameters. By avoiding code duplication, we keep our code clean and prevent maintenance problems.

4.3 Working with Generic Types

Just like generic functions, generic types solve a similar problem.

Generic types can work with any type and not just with a particular class, structure, or enumeration. That's why the built-in Swift collection types—the Array, the Set, and the Dictionary—are implemented as generic collections.

Let's say that we need a wrapper that holds values of various types: strings, integers, dates, etc. Without generics, we'd end up having a wrapper for each type: StringWrapper for String types, IntWrapper for Integers, and DateWrapper for dates.

```
struct StringWrapper {
    var storage: String
}

struct IntWrapper {
    var storage: Int
}

struct DateWrapper {
    var storage: Date
}
```

The number of dedicated wrapper types increases with each new type we need to support. Additionally, every added type means more code duplication. The code becomes a maintenance nightmare. Even choosing the right wrapper type is challenging.

Generics are here to help us!

Let's remove these wrappers and start implementing our generic solution. We define a wrapper structure that can work with any type.

```
struct Wrapper<T> {}
```

The placeholder appears right after the type's name within angled bracket. This placeholder type can be then used anywhere within the type's definition.

Now we're going to use it to define the storage property.

```
struct Wrapper<T> {
    var storage: T
```

Let's also add an initializer that takes an argument of placeholder type. This is going to initialize our storage property.

```
struct Wrapper<T> {
    var storage: T
    init(_ value: T) {
        storage = value
    }
}
```

Using the generic version is straightforward. Create a constant called piWrapped and initialize it with the value Double.pi.

```
let piWrapped = Wrapper<Double>(Double.pi)
```

In most cases, we can even skip the placeholder type. The compiler is able to figure out the type based on the provided value.

```
let piWrapped = Wrapper(Double.pi)
```

Next, we'll create a new instance that wraps a string. We won't provide the type, but let the Swift's type inference engine figure out the type based on the value, which is a String.

```
let stringWrapped = Wrapper("POP")
```

It also works with an object of type Date:

```
let dateWrapped = Wrapper(Date())
```

We can apply type constraints to generic types. To define a type constraint, place a class or protocol after the placeholder type separated by a colon.

For example, we could limit the Wrapper type to values that adopt the Equatable protocol.

```
struct Wrapper<T: Equatable> {}
```

Now, the Wrapper structure will be able to wrap only types that conform to the Equatable protocol. The playground will compile without problems since all the types we used—Double, String, and Date—conform to Equatable.

4.4 Placeholder Types in Protocols

So far, we've looked at the benefits of generic types and functions and how to use them. How about generics and protocols?

The TaggedData protocol defines requirements for any type that can hold binary data and uses a tag to identify it.

```
protocol TaggedData {
    var tag: String {get}
    var data: Data { get }
    init(tag: String, data: Data)
}
```

Now, wouldn't it be great to create a protocol that's not restricted to the Data type? Swift lets us declare placeholder types in protocols.

First, we'll rename the protocol to TaggedContent to express that it's not restricted to Data types.

```
protocol TaggedContent {
```

Next we declare an associated type. The associatedtype keyword lets us define a placeholder name for a type. The actual type is unknown until a conforming type provides it.

```
    associatedtype content
```

Now, replace the type of the data property with the placeholder type.

```
    var data: Content { get }
```

Finally, we refactor the initializer. The type of the data argument should be of Content type.

```
    init(tag: String, data: Content)
```

Now, we can create some adopting types. Let's start with the TaggedDouble structure. It adopts the TaggedContent protocol:

```
struct TaggedDouble: TaggedContent {
```

We need to provide the missing properties: for tag we set the type to String, and for data, we set the type to Double.

```
struct TaggedDouble: TaggedContent {
    var tag: String
```

```
    var data: Double
}
```

The next type is a struct that's going to provide the type Date for the data property.

```
struct TaggedDate: TaggedContent {
    var tag: String
    var data: Date
}
```

TaggedDate adopts TaggedContent. The tag property is a String, and the data property has the type Date.

We could create further structures or classes and assign any built-in or custom type to the given data property.

4.5 Using Generics with Protocols

We can also define generic types that adopt the TaggedContent protocol.

Let's create a generic structure called GenericTagged by providing the placeholder type. This structure adopts the TaggedContent protocol:

```
struct GenericTagged<T>: TaggedContent {}
```

GenericTagged has the same properties as our original structure, but we set the content type to the T generic placeholder.

```
struct GenericTagged<T>: TaggedContent {
    var tag: String
    var data: T
}
```

We'll provide the actual type when creating an instance of this generic structure.

Let's create a constant called taggedDouble, which is of type GenericTagged. And we can provide the type—say, Double—between angled brackets. Initialize it with a tag called "pi" and assign it the value of Double.pi.

```
let taggedDouble = GenericTagged<Double>(tag: "pi",
                                         data: Double.pi)
```

We can even omit the Double type because Swift's type inference engine can figure it out based on the value we provide.

```
let taggedDouble = GenericTagged(tag: "pi", data: Double.pi)
```

Using associated types with protocols couldn't be easier.

Note that we can also add type constraints to an associated type in the protocol. For example, we could restrict the data property to types that conform to Equatable.

```
protocol TaggedContent {
    associatedtype Content: Equatable
```

After this change, we need to update the GenericTagged structure as well. The placeholder type has to conform to the Equatable protocol. Now, the structure conforms to the TaggedContent protocol, and the compiler error is gone.

```
struct GenericTagged<T: Equatable>: TaggedContent {}
```

Generics are extremely useful, and Swift makes it easy for us to implement and use generic types and functions. We can also make our protocols work with associated types.

Protocol-oriented programming wouldn't be as flexible or elegant without generics.

4.6 Challenge: Implementing a Generic Stack

The stack is a sequential container that provides Last-In-First-Out (LIFO) access: new items gets pushed to the top of the stack, and the most recently added item can be accessed first.

The task is to implement a generic Stack that exposes the following methods and properties:

- `push(element)`: adds the element to the top of the stack
- `pop()`: returns and removes the top element from the stack; returns nil if the stack is empty
- `peek()`: returns the top element or nil if the stack is empty
- `count`: returns the number of elements in the stack
- `isEmpty`: returns a Boolean value indicating whether the stack has no elements

Hints:

- Start by defining the protocol.
- The `count` and `isEmpty` properties should be read-only.
- Methods that modify the instance should be declared as mutating
- Then, create the `Stack` type that adopts the protocol.
- You can use an array as the underlying storage.

Now give it a try. You can turn the page to check out my solution.

4.7 Solution

Hopefully, you managed to implement your array-based Stack. You can follow along with me and check out my solution.

First, we'll import the Foundation framework. We'll need it for the various built-in data types.

Now, let's define the public protocol conveniently named StackProtocol:

```
import Foundation

public protocol StackProtocol {
```

Our Stack needs to work with any type. Therefore, we'll introduce a placeholder type for the elements using the associatedtype keyword.

```
    associatedtype E
```

Next, we're going to define the method requirements. Let's start with the push() method. Pushing new elements into the stack's internal storage will modify the instance. Thus, we'll mark it with the mutating keyword.

```
    /// Adds the element to the top of the stack
    mutating func push(_ item: E)
```

The pop() method returns and removes the top element from the stack. This method should also be declared as mutating since it removes an element from the internal storage. pop() might return nil if the stack is empty. So, the return type should be an optional.

```
    /// Returns and removes the top element from the stack; returns nil if the stack is empty
    mutating func pop() -> E?
```

The peek() method returns the top element. However, since it doesn't remove the element from the stack, it doesn't need to be mutating. The return type is optional for the same reason as in the case of the pop() method.

```
    /// Returns the top element or nil if the stack is empty
    func peek() -> E?
```

The count property returns the number of elements in the stack. Its type is Integer, and it needs to be read-only—we don't want clients to change its value.

```
    /// Returns the number of elements in the stack
    var count: Int {get}
```

Finally, we'll add the isEmpty property. It returns a Boolean value and should be gettable, so clients can only read it:

```
    /// Returns a Boolean value indicating whether the stack has no elements
    var isEmpty: Bool {get}
}
```

Given this protocol, we'll create the Stack type as a public structure. It needs to be generic, so we provide the placeholder type T and have it adopt the StackProtocol:

```
public struct Stack<T>: StackProtocol {}
```

Next, we'll add the method and property requirements defined in the protocol. Let's copy them over from the protocol:

```
public struct Stack<T>: StackProtocol {
    /// Adds the element to the top of the stack
    mutating func push(_ item: E)

    /// Returns and removes the top element from the stack; returns nil if the stack is empty
    mutating func pop() -> E?

    /// Returns the top element or nil if the stack is empty
    func peek() -> E?

    /// Returns the number of elements in the stack
    var count: Int {get}

    /// Returns a Boolean value indicating whether the stack has no elements
    var isEmpty: Bool {get}
}
```

This code would trigger several compiler errors. First, we need to replace the associated type E with the placeholder type T.

Now we can start adding the missing implementations. Let's implement the push method:

```
    mutating func push(_ item: T) {
    }
```

This method adds a new element to the top of the Stack. We'll use an array to store the pushed elements. Clients shouldn't access the array directly, so we'll declare it as a private generic array:

```
    private var storage = [T]()
```

Now, we can finish the implementation of the push() method. First, let's make it public. We'll call the array's append() method to add the item to the storage:

```
    public mutating func push(_ item: T) {
        storage.append(item)
    }
```

The pop method returns the last element and removes it from the stack. The underlying storage is an array, which simplifies the implementation. We can call the Array popLast() instance method, which removes and returns the last element of the array:

```
    public mutating func pop() -> T? {
        storage.popLast()
    }
```

Note that I'm not using return here. Swift 5.1 no longer requires the return keyword in single-expression functions, but it's not a mistake if you add it.

The peek() method returns the top element without removing it. We'll rely on the array's last property to return the most recently-added element:

```
    public func peek() -> T? {
        storage.last
    }
```

What's left? The count property--it will simply return the array's count.

```
    public var count: Int {
        storage.count
    }
```

And finally, let's implement the isEmpty property, which returns the value of the array's matching property:

```
    public var isEmpty: Bool {
        storage.isEmpty
    }
```

We can use the Stack as follows:

```
var stringStack = Stack<String>()
stringStack.push("Hello")
stringStack.push(", ")
stringStack.push("Swift")
```

```
print(stringStack.pop() ?? "empty")
print(stringStack.pop() ?? "empty")
print(stringStack.peek() ?? "empty")
print(stringStack.count)
```

That's it! How does your solution compare to mine?

V. CASE STUDY - IMPLEMENTING AN APP USING POP

5.1 Weather App Design

Our goal is to implement a simple, yet functional Weather app using the principles of Protocol-Oriented Programming. The app will display weather information for a given location by getting the data using web services.

The Weather app follows the Model-View-ViewModel architecture. The MVVM architecture separates the user interface from business logic by introducing three components:

- → The View, which consists of visual elements: text fields, labels, switches, and so on. The View is concerned with tasks related to presenting the data, such as layout, font type, color, and animation
- → The ViewModel represents the state of the UI.
- → The Model is the application's state and defines the logic to manage that state

The View depends on the ViewModel, and the ViewModel has a reference to the Model. However, this dependency is unidirectional: the ViewModel doesn't hold a reference to the View, and the Model doesn't know about the ViewModel. The View is completely decoupled from the Model.

This design provides a clean separation of concerns and promotes testability and reusability.

The ViewModel propagates model changes to the View using connections called data bindings. With data bindings, the View reacts to ViewModel changes automatically, with no additional coding.

We're going to rely on SwiftUI and the Combine framework to implement the MVVM architecture. Here's a high-level overview of the WeatherApp's design:

- → The Views display the current weather information and allow the user to enter a location.
- → The ViewModel uses a data provider—the model—to fetch weather information. We'll make it conform to the ObservableObject protocol to enable data binding.
- → The Model component provides weather information. We're going to fetch weather data from the internet using web services.

We encapsulate the required initialization steps, network calls, and data conversions into dedicated controller types. We'll rely on built-in protocols to decode the JSON payloads.

So, this is our high-level design. Now, let's switch to Xcode.

5.2 Defining the UI Using SwiftUI

Open up Xcode and create a new iOS project. Select Single View App and enter "WeatherApp" as the product name. We'll use SwiftUI, and we're going to write Unit Tests, but we don't need Core Data or UI Tests. SwiftUI lets us lay out user interfaces in a declarative way.

Select the ContentView.swift file. There are two structures.

```
struct ContentView: View {
    var body: some View {
        Text("Hello, World!")
    }
}
```

ContentView conforms to the View protocol. The body property defines the view's content, layout, and behavior. The generated code has a Text view that displays "Hello, World!" as text output.

```
struct ContentView_Previews: PreviewProvider {
    static var previews: some View {
        ContentView()
    }
}
```

The ContentView_Previews structure conforms to the PreviewProvider protocol. Xcode uses the types that conform to the PreviewProvider protocol to generate previews. You can use Editor > Canvas to display the Canvas or press Option-Command-Enter. Press Resume to display the preview. The preview feature only works with macOS Catalina or newer macOS versions.

We're going to define the views of our app within the ContentView structure. The ContentView_Previews lets us check the UI without actually running the app.

Now, let's revisit our goal. We're building an app that retrieves the current weather for a location. The user interface will be clean and simple:

- → We'll use a TextField to enter the location's name
- → We display the weather information in a Text view

Delete the Text view and create a TextField:

```
struct ContentView: View {
    var body: some View {
        TextField(title, text: <#T##Binding<String>#>)
```

```
        //Text("Hello, World!")
    }
}
```

The TextField takes two parameters: a title and a binding. The title is the placeholder string. Let's display "Enter location." The second parameter is the binding.

```
        TextField("Enter location", text: <#T##Binding<String>#>)
```

A binding acts as a reference to a mutable state. It needs to refer to a property marked explicitly with the @State property wrapper.

This annotation tells SwiftUI to keep the value of the property throughout UI updates. When the state value changes, the view gets refreshed.

So, let's declare a state property:

```
struct ContentView: View {
    @State private var input: String = ""
```

It represents the text entered by the user in the text field, so I'm going to call it input. I marked it as private to avoid external components from accessing the view's state.

Now, finish the TextField initialization. We need to use the $ prefix to access a binding to a state variable:

```
    var body: some View {
        TextField("Enter location", text: $input)
```

Next, display the input string using a Text view:

```
    var body: some View {
        TextField("Enter location", text: $input)
        Text(input)
    }
```

Embed the two views in a vertical stack:

```
    var body: some View {
        VStack {
            TextField("Enter location", text: $input)
            Text(input)
        }
    }
```

If we run the app, it displays what we type and mirrors it in the text view.

Let's improve the appearance of our UI. Add a Divider between the text field and the text view:

```
VStack {
    TextField("Enter location", text: $input)
    Divider()
    Text(input)
}
```

This displays a horizontal line as a visual separator between the UI elements. And I set the textfield's font to the title text style, and the text view's text to a smaller, body font.

```
VStack {
    TextField("Enter city", text: $input)
        .font(.title)
    Divider()
    Text(input)
        .font(.body)
}.padding()
```

Finally, apply default padding to the entire vertical stack. This prevents our views from touching the edges of the main view. Let's hit run.

All right, it looks much better now. But we're not done yet. We'll return to this and add more logic once we implement the missing pieces.

5.3 The WebServiceController Protocol

By now we've implemented a basic UI for our app. The next logical step is to start feeding it with data.

So, let's continue with the model layer. We'll be relying on web services to retrieve accurate weather information. There are various weather web services available, both free and paid.

We're going to use two web services, provided by OpenWeatherMap.org and WeatherStack.com. Both services return their response in JSON format - but the payload's structure and contents are different.

Although the APIs are incompatible, we need to integrate them seamlessly into our application.

We'll start by creating a service protocol that defines the common method and the expected results and errors. Then, we'll define dedicated controllers for each web service. These controllers need to expose the API defined by the service protocol. Thus, we won't have to deal with different, incompatible interfaces in our application code.

Now, let's go back to Xcode, and create a new group called "Model." Here I add a new Swift file that will hold the definition of the service protocol. Save it as "WebServiceController.swift."

Create a public protocol with the same name:

```swift
public protocol WebServiceController {}
```

We need a method for fetching the weather information. Let's call it fetchWeatherData.

```swift
func fetchWeatherData(
```

The method needs a parameter to allow callers to provide the name of the city—of type String:

```swift
func fetchWeatherData(for city: String,
```

The method is supposed to fetch data from the internet. Such long-running tasks should be implemented as asynchronous methods.

Swift makes it easy to implement asynchronous behavior. Instead of returning a value, we use a completion handler. Completion handlers are blocks of code that get executed when the asynchronous method finishes.

```
func fetchWeatherData(for city: String,
                      completionHandler:
```

The method should return a description of the current weather conditions for the specified location. To keep it simple, let's use a String. It is optional because we might not always receive a valid response.

```
func fetchWeatherData(for city: String,
                      completionHandler: (String?,
```

Speaking of issues, the completion handler should also include an error. Various problems may occur, since we're accessing the network after all.

It's a good habit to create dedicated error types that are specific to the given context. In Swift, we can model related error conditions using enumerations.

Create a public enumeration called WebServiceControllerError. I make it adopt the Error protocol. The Error protocol doesn't define any requirements; however, by conforming to it, we make it clear that our enumeration represents an error.

```
public enum WebServiceControllerError: Error {
}
```

Since the Error protocol doesn't dictate any method or property requirements, it leaves us a lot of room for creativity.

Let's try to cover the main issues that might occur. First, we might have an invalid URL. So I'm going to add a case for it. The invalidURL() case includes the URL string as an associated value.

```
public enum WebServiceControllerError: Error {
    case invalidURL(String)
}
```

The returned response could also be invalid. For example, the JSON payload may be malformed, or the server might return an HTML page instead of a JSON string. To report such issues, I introduce the invalidPayload() case.

```
    case invalidPayload(URL)
}
```

This case includes the original fetch URL. By providing the URL, callers can identify the origin of the unexpected content.

And finally, for everything else, I use a generic case called forwarded(). The forwarded case includes the original error.

```
    case forwarded(Error)
}
```

Now that we have a dedicated error, let's complete the declaration of the fetchWeatherData() method. The error is optional; upon successful completion it will be nil:

```
func fetchWeatherData(for city: String,
        completionHandler: (String?, WebServiceControllerError?)
        -> Void)
```

And this is the final signature of our fetchWeatherData() method.

We established the mapping between the web service calls and the rest of our application. Now it's time to integrate our first real weather API.

5.4 Working with Third-Party API

We're going to fetch real weather data using the OpenWeatherMap web service.

Open https://openweathermap.org and navigate to the API page. For our app, we're only interested in the current weather data. Let's see its documentation. We'll use the API that returns weather data by city name.

```
api.openweathermap.org/data/2.5/weather?q={city name}
```

The syntax is simple. We must provide the city name and the API key as query parameters:

```
http://api.openweathermap.org/data/2.5/find?q=\(city)&units=imperial&appid=\(API.key)
```

To make it work, you'll need an API key. To obtain the key, you'll need to sign up. The process is straightforward, and the steps are described in the "How to start" section. After registration, it takes a couple of hours until the API key is activated.

So, please go ahead and get that set up, and we'll pick up in the next section.

5.5 Implementing the OpenWeatherMapController

In this section, we integrate the OpenWeatherMap API and fetch live weather information.

We first need a new file - create it in the Model group and name it OpenWeatherMapController.swift.

Let's declare the class next. OpenWeatherMapController adopts the WebServiceController protocol:

```
class OpenWeatherMapController: WebServiceController {}
```

Xcode generates the required method declaration:

```
    func fetchWeatherData(for city: String,
                          completionHandler: @escaping (String?,
WebServiceControllerError?) -> Void) {
```

First, we configure the web service endpoint. Let's have a look at the API documentation at https://openweathermap.org/current.

We're going to use the API that accepts unit parameters. Search for "Units format". Here's the API call we're looking for:

```
api.openweathermap.org/data/2.5/find?q=London&units=imperial
```

Create a constant called endpoint, and assign it the string we just copied:

```
let endpoint = "api.openweathermap.org/data/2.5/find?q=London&units=imperial"
```

We need to make a couple of changes to create a URL out of this string. First, let's make it a valid URL by prepending https://.

```
let endpoint = "https://api.openweathermap.org/data/2.5/find?q=\(city)&units=imperial&appid=\(API.key)"
```

And replace "London" with the value of the city argument.

```
let endpoint = "https://api.openweathermap.org/data/2.5/find?q=\(city)&units=imperial"
```

We also have to supply the API key. I created an enumeration that holds the key as a static string. This is a convenient way to define our constants.

```
private enum API {
    static let key = "<your_key_here>"
}
```

You should paste your own OpenWeatherMaps key here. As mentioned in the previous section, you can obtain an API key after a quick registration.

So let's also add the appid parameter and assign it the generated API.key.

```
let endpoint = "https://api.openweathermap.org/data/2.5/find?q=\
(city)&units=imperial&appid=\(API.key)"
```

The city argument may contain invalid characters. I create a safe URL by calling the addingPercentEncoding() String instance method. The characters should belong to the URL query allowed character set.

I used the guard statement to catch potential issues.

```
        guard let safeURLString = endpoint.addingPercentEncod-
ing(withAllowedCharacters: CharacterSet.urlQueryAllowed),
```

If the safeURLString is created, we can try to instantiate the endpoint URL:

```
        let endpointURL = URL(string: safeURLString) else {
```

If any of these calls fail, invoke the completion handler with nil for weather description, with the error is set to invalidURL() and with the endpoint set as associated value.

```
            completionHandler(nil, WebServiceControllerError.in-
validURL(endpoint))
```

Here we get a compiler error:

```
Escaping closure captures non-escaping parameter 'completionHan-
dler'
```

A closure is said to escape a function if it gets called after the function returns.

The compiler is right, since the method returns before the actual network call completes. Thus, the closure escapes the fetchWeatherData method body. A closure that is passed as an argument or function is non-escaping by default. We need to mark it explicitly with @escaping to indicate that it is allowed to escape.

We need to change the method's signature both in the protocol and in this class.

```
    func fetchWeatherData(for city: String,
```

```
                    completionHandler: @escaping (String?,
WebServiceControllerError?) -> Void) {
```

Next up, we'll implement the networking part.

5.6 Completing the OpenWeatherMapController

Let's continue the implementation of the OpenWeatherMapController. For networking we'll use a URLSession data task. I use the initializer that takes a URL and a completion handler:

```
let dataTask = URLSession.shared.dataTask(with: endpointURL, completionHandler: { (data, response, error) -> Void in
```

The URL is our endpoint and we're going to implement the completion handler. We have a data parameter, a response and an error. If there's an error, we're going to wrap it in our dedicated error type and pass it back to the caller.

So let's check whether there was an error. It should be nil or else we call our completion handler.

```
    guard error == nil else {
        completionHandler(nil, WebServiceControllerError.forwarded(error!))
```

If the returned response is nil, we invoke the completion handler and provide the invalidPayload error.

```
    guard let responseData = data else {
        completionHandler(nil, WebServiceControllerError.invalidPayload(endpointURL))
```

Next we're going to process the response. Parsing JSON data is beyond the scope of this book. The JSON Data > Swift mappings are defined in the OpenWeatherMapData swift file.

I'm going to add it to our project. Right-click on the Model group > Add files, and select the JSONMappers folder. The corresponding group gets created and the file with the Codable structures is added to the project.

The following snippet contains the data-parsing logic. It creates a JSON decoder, and uses it to decode the JSON response into the corresponding Swift structures.

If the decoding succeeds, we pass in the weather description to the completion handler. Otherwise, we call the completion handler with the appropriate error.

```
            // decode json
            let decoder = JSONDecoder()
            do {
                let weatherList = try decoder.decode(OpenWeathe
```

```
MapContainer.self, from: responseData)
                guard let weatherInfo = weatherList.list?.first,
                    let weather = weatherInfo.weather.first?.main,
                    let temperature = weatherInfo.main.temp else {
                    completionHandler(nil, WebServiceControl-
lerError.invalidPayload(endpointURL))
                    return
                }
                // compose weather information
                let weatherDescription = "\(weather) \(tempera-
ture) °F"
                completionHandler(weatherDescription, nil)
            } catch let error {
                completionHandler(nil, WebServiceControllerError.
forwarded(error))
            }
```

And, last but not least, let's not forget to call

```
dataTask.resume()
```

5.7 Introducing the ViewModel

We can now fetch current weather data using the OpenWeatherMap service. And we've also got the user interface. So, let's connect the dots.

The missing piece is the ViewModel. It acts as padding between the Model and the View, without referencing the View.

We'll introduce a new class that represents the ViewModel. First, add a new group: ViewModel. Then, create a new swift file called WeatherViewModel.swift.

Now, let's declare the ViewModel class. WeatherViewModel adopts the ObservableObject protocol to enable data binding.

```
class WeatherViewModel: ObservableObject {
```

Next, I declare a property called weatherInfo and initialize it to an empty string.

```
    @Published var weatherInfo = ""
```

By marking it with @Published property wrapper, we allow SwiftUI to observe this property and update the View whenever this property changes.

```
    @Published var weatherInfo = ""
```

The ViewModel exposes a method to fetch the weather information. It relies on the model—that is, the OpenWeatherMapController—to provide this functionality. Let's create a private property weatherService and initialize it:

```
    private let weatherService = OpenWeatherMapController()
```

Next, add the method that fetches the current weather for a given city. fetch has a parameter called city of type String:

```
    func fetch(city: String) {
```

We'll use the weatherService fetchWeatherData method.

```
        weatherService.fetchWeatherData(for: city, completionHandler: { (info, error) in
```

Error handling comes next. The error should be nil, and the returned weather information needs to be valid. Otherwise, we update the weatherInfo property with an error message and exit the method.

```
            guard error == nil,
                let weatherInfo = info else {
```

```
            DispatchQueue.main.async {
                self.weatherInfo = "Could not retrieve weather
information for \(city)"
                return
            }
        }
```

As you may remember, changing the @Published property triggers UI updates. Since the completion handler executes in the background, it is crucial to switch to the main UI thread whenever we update the weatherInfo property.

If the weather data has been fetched successfully, we can assign it to the published property. Again, we need to perform this update in the main UI thread:

```
            DispatchQueue.main.async {
                self.weatherInfo = weatherInfo
            }
        })
    }
}
```

We're done with the ViewModel. Next, we need to make some adjustments in our View.

5.8 Presenting Weather Data

By now, we've implemented the Model and the ViewModel. In this section, we're going to add the missing link that allows the View to reflect changes in the Model.

The ViewModel conforms to the ObservableObject protocol, and has a @Published property. SwiftUI can automatically monitor @Published properties for changes and notify the views that rely on the modified data.

Let's switch to the ContentView. We need to tell SwiftUI which type has the data it should observe. As we know, that's the WeatherViewModel class. Let's create a new property weatherViewModel and initialize it:

```
var weatherViewModel = WeatherViewModel()
```

To allow SwiftUI to observe the published properties, we've got to mark the property using the @ObservedObject property wrapper. Bear in mind that you can only use @ObservedObject with types that conform to the ObservableObject protocol.

```
@ObservedObject var weatherViewModel = WeatherViewModel()
```

And we're done with the data binding part.

Next, update the Text view to display the weatherViewModel's weatherInfo instead of the input text:

```
Text("\(weatherViewModel.weatherInfo)")
```

Whenever the published data changes, the view gets updated. There's only one thing left: we need to trigger the fetching of weather information and pass in the city name entered by the user.

I'm going to change the TextField's initializer.

```
TextField("Enter city", text: $input)
```

We'll use TextField(onEditingChanged:, onCommit:). I leave the onEditingChanged: closure empty. The onCommit closure get called when the user hits the return key.

```
TextField("Enter city", text: $input, onEditingC-
hanged: { (_) in
        }) {
```

Let's check if there was a valid input. If the user provided some text, call the weatherViewModel's fetch() method.

```
if !self.input.isEmpty {
    self.weatherViewModel.fetch(city: self.input)
}
}
```

Note that we're not returning the weather information. The fetch method updates the published weatherInfo property, which in turn will automatically update the Text view.

Let's run the app. Excellent! We have a functional weather application!

5.9 Challenge: Adding A Fallback Service

I added a new Web Service controller that allows us to fetch weather information using the WeatherStack API.

The corresponding Codable structures can be found in the JSONMappers group.

Note that I had to add the WeatherStack domain to the App Transport Security whitelist. The free plan doesn't allow us to use an https connection, and the iOS security policy denies http connections by default. To use the web service, WeatherStack must be included in the exception domain list.

Your task is to implement a fallback strategy. If the OpenWeatherMap web service call fails, fall back to the WeatherStack service.

Hints:

→ Add a new initializer requirement to the WebServiceController protocol. The initializer takes an optional WebServiceController parameter that can be used to pass in a fallback service.

→ Also add a computed property requirement. This property represents the fallbackService and should be gettable. The fallbackService can be nil.

→ Next, implement the new initializer and property requirement in the conforming types.

→ Invoke the fallback service's fetchWeatherData() method from the data task's completion handler if the call returns an error or the payload is invalid.

→ Finally, make sure to set the OpenWeatherMapController's fallback service when initializing it in the WeatherViewModel. The fallback service should be a WeatherStack instance. The WeatherStack shouldn't have a fallback service.

All right, give it a try. Turn the page to check out my solution when you're ready (or if you get stuck).

5.10 Solution

Welcome back! Hopefully you've managed to come up with an elegant solution. Let me show you one way to approach this problem.

Here's the WebServiceController:

```
public protocol WebServiceController {
```

I'll add the initializer requirement first. The fallbackService parameter is a WebServiceController, and it's optional, allowing callers to set it to nil, which indicates that the controller doesn't have a fallback service.

```
    init(fallbackService: WebServiceController?)
```

The fallbackService computed property is of type WebServiceController and it can be nil, so I make it optional.

```
    var fallbackService: WebServiceController? { get }
```

Next, we'll switch to the OpenWeatherMapController. Let's add the fallbackService property first. By declaring it as a constant we make it immutable. Thus, we can only assign its initial value during initialization. After that, it can't be modified further.

```
final class OpenWeatherMapController: WebServiceController {
    let fallbackService: WebServiceController?
```

Next comes the initializer. I provide a default nil value for the fallbackService parameter.

```
    init(fallbackService: WebServiceController? = nil) {
        self.fallbackService = fallbackService
    }
```

We'll incorporate the fallback logic into the fetchWeatherData method.

```
    func fetchWeatherData(for city: String,
                          completionHandler: @escaping (String?,
WebServiceControllerError?) -> Void) {
```

Let's have a look at the data task's completion handler. We might receive an error, so let's cover this case first.

```
let dataTask = URLSession.shared.dataTask(with: endpointURL, completionHandler: { (data, response, error) -> Void in
```

If the error is not nil, we'll try to use the fallback service—instead of calling the completion handler with the forwarded error:

```
        guard error == nil else {
            if let fallback = self.fallbackService {
                fallback.fetchWeatherData(for: city, comple-
tionHandler: completionHandler)
```

If there's no fallback service, we have no other choice but tp return the error to the caller via the completion handler.

```
            } else {
                completionHandler(nil, WebServiceControl-
lerError.forwarded(error!))
            }
            return
        }
```

We'll apply the same logic if the returned data is nil:

```
        guard let responseData = data else {
            if let fallback = self.fallbackService {
                fallback.fetchWeatherData(for: city, comple-
tionHandler: completionHandler)
            } else {
                completionHandler(nil, WebServiceControl-
lerError.invalidPayload(endpointURL))
            }
            return
        }

        // decode json
```

We'll repeat the process for the WeatherStackMapController class. First, we'll add the fallbackService property.

```
final class WeatherStackController: WebServiceController {
    let fallbackService: WebServiceController?
```

Next, we'll define the initializer. I provide a nil default value for the fallbackService argument:

```
final class WeatherStackController: WebServiceController {
    init(fallbackService: WebServiceController? = nil) {
        //
    }
```

And let's integrate the fallback logic by copying over the code from the

OpenWeatherMapController class.

We'll make some final adjustment in the ViewModel. To use the fallback strategy, we'll pass in a WeatherStackController instance to the OpenWeatherMapController initializer.

```
class WeatherViewModel: ObservableObject {
    @Published var weatherInfo = ""

    private let weatherService = OpenWeatherMapController(fall-
backService: WeatherStackController())
```

The WeatherStackController doesn't have a fallback service. However, since the design is flexible, we could add a third web service and use it as a fallback for the WeatherStackController, and so on.

CONCLUSION

6.1 Next Steps

I hope you enjoyed the book, and now you've got a taste for how powerful protocols can be. If you found this book useful, please leave a nice review or rating.

If you're interested in more Swift content, check out my other books in the Swift Clinic series:

- → "Design Patterns in Swift 5" explores the Gang of Four's software design patterns and shows how to implement them in modern Swift.
- → "Machine Learning with Core ML 2 and Swift" teaches you how to integrate machine learning into your apps using hands-on Swift coding examples.
- → "Introduction to Algorithms and Data Structures in Swift" aims to help you write better and faster code.

Feel free to visit my website at https://www.leakka.com for free goodies and updates on future books and courses.

Thank you!

6.2 Useful Links

As an instructor, my goal is to share my 25+ years of software development expertise.

My books are available on Amazon amazon.com/author/nyisztor and iTunes https://itunes.apple.com/us/author/karoly-nyisztor/id1345964804?mt=11.

Check out my courses on:

- → Teachable: https://learnwithkarl.teachable.com
- → Udemy: https://www.udemy.com/user/karolynyisztor/
- → LinkedIn Learning: https://www.linkedin.com/learning/instructors/karoly-nyisztor?u=2125562
- → Pluralsight: https://www.pluralsight.com/profile/author/karoly-nyisztor

Check out these links for free tutorials, blog posts, and other useful stuff:

- → https://www.leakka.com
- → https://www.youtube.com/@LearnWithKarl
- → https://github.com/nyisztor
- → https://x.com/knyisztor

www.ingramcontent.com/pod-product-compliance
Lightning Source LLC
Chambersburg PA
CBHW030442220526
45464CB00006B/2385